"The highest compliment one can give a fellow pastor is to say that he is truly a man of God. Dr. Derek Grier is the consummate man of God. He is meek and humble, yet dynamic and inspiring. A pastor and teacher, Grier is articulate, gracious and anointed to lead ʼ ers of Grace Christian Church where he is herd. Dr. Grier is also a gifted leader is deftly leading a group of over J prayer and fellowship. He ha   of encouragement to me becaι   ᴜ desire to see the unification of the b

— .vid N. Hunter
Tribe of ̣ ah Miracle Center
Church of God in Christ
Woodbridge, Virginia

"Dr. Grier is a man deeply rooted in the Word of God. His commitment to the authority of Scripture is manifest in his insightful teaching and preaching, his profound life of prayer and his faithful engagement with the issues of our culture."

—Rev. John Guernsey
Senior Pastor, All Saints' Episcopal Church
Woodbridge, Virginia

"At a time when our society is in desperate need of spiritual direction, Dr. Grier has emerged as one of the most outstanding spiritual leaders in the community. Like the prophet Daniel, Derek is a man of godly wisdom and genuine compassion for the cause of the Gospel. His bold determination, perseverance and kind demeanor serve as an example to all men and women of faith."

—Rev. Don Sampson
Senior Pastor, Crossroads Presbyterian Church (PCA)
Dumfries, Virginia

"When I'm around Dr. Grier, I feel the presence of God. He seems to radiate God's Spirit in both word and action!"

—Rev. Rick Veit
St. Margaret's Episcopal Church
Woodbridge, Virginia

"I would gladly say to readers of Dr. Grier's book that this man of God is a gifted leader for Grace Christian Church and all the churches in Eastern Prince William County. The foundation for Dr. Grier's leadership is prayer. I believe everyone will be blessed by getting to know Derek's heart for God through his book and in person."

—Rev. Larry Craddock
Pastor, Dumfries United Methodist Church
Dumfries, Virginia

"I have always been impressed that Dr. Grier is a man of prayer. He is also a man of God who has willingly made himself accountable to his peers. He has been and continues to be a source of encouragement to me personally."

—Rev. Dick Delap
Pastor, Open Heart Community Church
Woodbridge, Virginia

"Dr. Grier is a unique individual whose effective lines of communication extend from the house of faith into the community at large."

—Dave Mabie
Clerk of Court
Prince William County, Virginia

"I appreciate Derek Grier's dedication and steadfastness in the ministry. His love for God shines through in all he does. Dr. Grier's accomplishment in writing this book is just another example of how he stays focused on God and His plan for his life. I know that God will use this book to bless many."

—Rev. Shelby Boldt
Executive Director, Hylton Memorial
Chapel Christian Event Center
Woodbridge, Virginia

"Dr. Grier's personal commitment to prayer, sanctification and the study of the Word of God has certainly made this story teller's fresh ideas shine on the pages of this book. His keen insight, understanding of Scripture and teaching style makes clear the message God intends for this generation of believers. Derek is a bridge builder who understands that our Lord has given us all the ministry of reconciliation. I know the Lord will receive all the glory from this effort."

—Dr. William Wright, Ph.D.
Pastor Emmanuel Bible Fellowship
Dumfries, Virginia

STILL STANDING

Insights Into the Life of the Prophet Daniel

DEREK GRIER

CREATION
HOUSE PRESS

STILL STANDING by Derek Grier
Published by Creation House Press
A part of Strang Communications Company
600 Rinehart Road
Lake Mary, Florida 32746
www.creationhouse.com

Unless otherwise noted, Scripture quotations are from The Holy Bible, New International version, © 1973, 1978, 1984 by the International Bible Society. Used by permission.

Scripture quotations marked KJV are from the King James Version of the Bible.

Cover design by Karen Gonsalves
Interior design by David Bilby

Library of Congress Control Number: 2002114911

International Standard Book Numbers:
0-88419-973-8 — Paperback Edition
1-59185-212-9 — Hardback Edition

Printed in the United States of America.
03 04 05 06   8 7 6 5 4 3 2 1

DEDICATION

*To my two boys, Derek Jr. and David—
Always be true to your God and your
conscience. Grow into strong, faithful
and fearless men. Never let anyone
influence you to become less than what
God has intended you to be.*

*To my wife, Yeromitou—Honey, as we
approach our tenth wedding anniver-
sary, I realize more than ever that you
are the wind beneath my wings. You
are the inspiration to 1,000 love songs
not yet sung. I love you dearly.*

*To Karen Prewitt—Thank you for your
faithful administration over the years.
You are a pearl of great price.*

FOREWORD

The desire to achieve and succeed is inherent in the heart of all humans no matter their socio-economic status. However, only a small percentage of the world's population will experience the level of success desired. This lack of personal achievement is due in some cases to lack of opportunity, disadvantaged situations and external resources restrictions. However, in the majority of the cases, people fail to achieve their God-given purpose and potential due to their ignorance of or failure to effectively apply the eternal principles and laws of life established by the Creator.

Life was designed for success and created for you to achieve and experience God's destiny and vision for you. But life was also designed to function according to set laws and principles that guarantee success. If we can learn and apply these laws as laid down by the creator of life, success will be inevitable and will take us from being victims to experiencing the joy of victory.

Dr. Derek Grier, in this work, *Still Standing*, breaks these fundamental principles down for all of us to apply through the time-tested lessons embedded in the life and words of the Hebrew Prophet, Daniel. Using the skill of a surgeon and the passion of a father, Derek takes account of Daniel in his

Babylonian Exile, and brings it to life in a way that makes it a contemporary experience. *Still Standing* captivates the spirit of life in the times of Daniel, and transports us to a time where we feel like we are living with this great character of history. Derek then distills the vital principles from the source of all wisdom—the Bible—and shows how we can learn to live a life of uncompromising integrity and standard in a world of accommodation and compromise

Still Standing is destined to become a classic and perhaps the foundation of a movie for the world to experience. I dare you to open the following pages and relive the life of a man whose unwavering faith will inspire you to stand in the face of your temptations to compromise. This is an excellent work.

—Dr. Myles Munroe
Nassau, Bahamas

PREFACE

The use of the term "prophet" tends to conjure up images of a hermit, dressed in austere clothing, with deep frown lines etched into his cheerless face. He is moody and petulant, constantly ranting dark sayings that no one can completely understand. Such misconceptions about these men are the reason that the prophetic books of the Bible are the least read section of the entire cannon.

No matter how many times I read the prophets, I find a fresh appreciation for them each time. The keys that have helped me unlock these books of the Bible are basic. While reading the scriptures, I am constantly asking three questions: What does the text mean? What did it mean to the original audience? Then the most important question—how does this scripture apply to my life and circumstances? Because of this last question, it was only natural to weave my own experience into the telling of Daniel's.

Daniel has become a source of great personal encouragement to me, as he soon will be to you. *Still Standing* is the first in a series designed to bring to life the personalities behind the Bible's prophetic writings. You will begin to see yourself in their experiences, understand their passions and be able to apply their lessons to your own life.

CONTENTS

CHAPTER 1

THE ROYAL FOOD

It seems as if I am dreaming. When will I awake from this madness?

For miles around me, all I see is rubble and smoke. Everything is still, but in the stillness I can hear quiet moans that sometimes are punctuated by sporadic, piercing cries of rage.

My hands won't stop shaking. My heart flutters like a bird darting within a bamboo cage. I can hear myself swallow—as if my ears are inside my head. I feel my lungs expanding with every breath. My feet shake, even when I am still.

My mind is working in slow motion, and all I can think about is whether or not Grandpa is still alive. I arrive at his house. The front door is off the hinge.

I enter his room, and I fall to my knees when I see

his eyes staring vacantly toward the ceiling. The beautiful lines that used to spring from the corners of his smiling eyes are gone, and his countenance is blank. His body lies cold and lifeless on his matted bed.

"Poppy!" I cry.

Grandma puts her hands on my shoulders and wearily kneels to look me in the eye.

"He's with Abraham now," she says.

I bite my lip and try not to cry. Dark clouds are blowing violently in my soul, which is nearly bursting from pressure.

I fight my tears, but my jaw grows tense, and I feel a trickle of blood running from my lip to my chin. Its acrid taste seems appropriate for this moment. My throat tightens as I swallow bitter reality.

I look up to heaven to yell, "*Why?*" but before I can open my mouth, I recall the voice of Jeremiah, the Weeping Prophet, warning us of this day.

But we stopped listening to prophets a long time ago.

My name is Daniel. The year is 597 B.C. Zedekiah, the king of Judah, has been captured, and Nebuchadnezzar, the king of Babylon, has broken down our city walls and laid our nation to waste.

Centuries Later

Two thousand six hundred years later, a young minister studies the life of Daniel to find strength. He meets with him through the reading of Old Testament scriptures and finds in the young Jew a companion for his own journey of faith.

In the mid-1990s, one more storefront church was added to the red-light district of Washington, D.C. The name *Song of Faith Church* was stretched in white lettering across the faded red awning, and I was the little church's new pastor.

A handful of founding members and I spent weeks cleaning out the grime, while painting, hanging drywall and otherwise getting our 1,000 square-foot church ready to pass zoning inspections. We built a stage and purchased a pulpit. And although our air-conditioners didn't work, it didn't stop us from being ready for our first service—which took place in the heat of a very hot summer in the city.

Over the next two years the church grew to about thirty regular attendees. We had a few college students—but mostly ex-addicts, ex-convicts and homeless men attended. On occasion we filled the 50-seat sanctuary, but seldomly.

Despite the sparsely filled seats, our mid-week service was spirited. Often I would have to raise my voice to distract my congregation from the sound of rats scurrying against the building's tin-plated ceilings—though even the ever-busy rodents seemed to have a spiritual streak. Some Sunday mornings they would come from behind the walls and join us for service.

Exciting though our beginning was, church life wasn't without its challenges. Before every meeting we would have to sweep away the empty crack vials, needle cases and dirt that had accumulated in front of the door since the last time we had met. Iron security bars were mounted everywhere. At times I wasn't sure if those bars were there to keep undesirables out or to keep us in.

We loved meeting the needs of people, but maintaining the church was a tremendous burden. The weekly offerings were as dismal as the surroundings, and it wasn't long before I was forced to borrow money to pay the rent for the building.

I was facing challenges in my personal life as well.

During these early days of our church, my first son was born. About four years earlier—just before my wife, Yeromitou, and I married—I had started having pain at the base of my spine whenever I sat for too long.

I underwent a very painful surgery to correct the matter. It was unsuccessful. I was feeling sick most of the time, and I would have to kneel instead of sit at my desk to work. My marriage was feeling the weight of this challenge.

In addition, before I began the church, I had become something of a spiritual outcast. People had prophesied my personal destruction—even my death. I had reached a point in which it seemed as if their prophecies were coming true.

Maybe I am cursed, I would think. Thoughts like these that I had tried so desperately to stall would flood my mind with what felt like irresistible force. Everything in the city seemed so big, but my church and resources were so small. I felt mocked by the historic government buildings that I passed on my way to my little church. I started to believe that I was a failure.

Into the Crucible

The youthful Daniel prepares for what will become the journey of his life. As he will learn, this is God's will for him, but it is going to cost Daniel much more than he ever wanted to pay.

We hear that soon we will be forced to make the 1,000-mile journey from Israel to Babylon. We are hungry, tired and distraught, yet the unthinkable—captivity in a foreign land—is still to come.

My younger sister no longer looks me in the eye. She knows I saw the Babylonian soldiers drag her from the house into the woods. Ma cried that whole night. Dad seemed to age twenty years in a matter of hours. She returned with her garments torn and dirty from her fight—and from the assault. Her face was bruised, and her neck was bloody. Little sister no longer smiles.

Dad speaks to me with great intention. It is as if he is trying to shove a lifetime of lessons into his every word. A few minutes ago he told me that if something should happen to him I was to make sure my little sister finds a good husband.

He knows more than he is saying. Sometimes he

avoids eye contact with me. I think it is because he knows I can see the fear in his eyes. He tells us things will get better after our resettlement in Babylon. Our people survived Pharaoh, he says reassuringly, and somehow we'll make it under the hand of Nebuchadnezzar as well.

Mom, on the other hand, keeps saying everything will be all right even though I often catch her staring at me in a way that makes me think she believes otherwise. When she hugs me, she smells my hair, as if she might capture it forever in her breath. Last night she slept while holding my sister between her and Dad.

Our long march has begun. We have moved north from Judah, and in just a few minutes we will be paraded through the streets of Riblah, a stronghold of Babylon just north of Israel. Maybe I will get a glimpse of the monster, King Nebuchadnezzar. He has called for our captured king, Zedekiah, to be brought before him and is sure to make a public spectacle of our defeated leader.

I know he soon will call for the nobles of Israel to do the same. My family is part of the noble class. In the meantime, all of us are forced to watch as Nebuchadnezzar humiliates our king by making him bow before him.

I notice that the Babylonian monarch seems to be looking in my direction. He's staring my way. Maybe if I smile at him, he will spare my parents. I force a kind expression on my face, but Nebuchadnezzar continues to look right through me.

As he glances away, he motions to his soldiers. Their blades flash in the sun, and in a moment, all of King Zedekiah's sons fall dead. Their blood begins to flow down the imperial white-marble steps.

Then the court crier shouts in Hebrew and Aramaic, "May this be the last thing the king of Judah sees!" With that, the soldiers gouged out our king's eyes. (See Jeremiah 39:6–7.)

Suddenly I see my parents are being taken!

Sister and I try to push through the crowd to see Mom and Dad. Will this be the last time? An older Jewish boy holds us back. Again we hear the sound of drawn swords, and we see blood streaming on white marble.

"Ma! Pa!" we cry, but there is no response. Only silence and the thud of lifeless bodies hitting the ground.

It's Over

It is the fall of 1984, and the young man has not yet become a minister. The first steps of his own painful journey—from disillusioned university student to chosen vessel of the one true God—are just beginning.

The day was as clear and bright as any other. I took the bus from my downtown dormitory apartment in Washington, D.C., to the Howard University campus with one of my "boys"—one of my peers—to start my morning courses. I was looking forward to getting them over with so I could go to the campus yard and hang out with some new girls. This was my routine. It was a very typical day for me.

I took my normal classroom seat next to the same set of friends and listened to the standard boring lecture. Shortly into the professor's discourse, my heart started beating fast. I began to feel a heaviness beyond words, and I became very self-conscious. It felt like I was unraveling from the inside out.

As soon as class was over, rather than hanging out as I had planned, I left campus to travel back to my dorm room. I tried to avoid eye contact with the other passengers on the bus. I did not want to talk to anyone. I just wanted to go to my dorm and sort things out.

I had chosen to attend Howard University because it is one of the best historically African American colleges around. I loved my people.

In time I had bought the belief promoted by certain quarters of my race that Christianity is a white man's religion and Islam is the true faith for people of color. I had just finished reading the Quran and planned to become a Muslim. I did not know that Mohammed thought of himself as a white man or the many other tragic racial views espoused by the religion. I was simply reacting to the pain of knowing that some of the people who used to sit under the cross on Sundays were the same ones who beat and raped my ancestors.

It was not very long ago that these people of the

cross turned police dogs and water hoses on us. For me, a mere two years had passed since I last was called "nigger."

When I got to my room, I lay on my bed. *Is this what it feels like to lose your mind?* I wondered. It just did not make sense—it was like I was feeling the desires of someone far greater than I. I was not from a religious background, but instinctively I knew that what I was feeling was of God. I could sense Him deeply yearning for a relationship with my people, and indirectly with me.

I couldn't fathom why I was having such feelings—which were like a groaning that I couldn't utter. Something or someone larger than me and my world had suffered loss and was letting me know. It was distress, like a mother must feel who has just received news that her child has been kidnapped, or a father must feel who has to visit his son behind bars.

As the feelings intensified, I fell from my bed to the floor. Suddenly I saw a man standing in a long, flowing gown. All He said was, "This is it." Without needing to ask, I knew the man was Jesus and that He was telling me to follow Him and that He loved me. His voice was so loud and sure that I ran and opened all the doors in my dorm room to see if one of my roommates was playing tricks on me. No one else was home.

By then the shock of what I was experiencing had worn off. I felt a sense of clarity I had never felt before. My experience that day made two things clear to me.

First, for the first time in my life I really understood that I was a sinner. The feeling of guilt I had had on campus was what Christians call "conviction."

Second, I learned that Jesus loved me and my people. God had to remove the racial barriers between me and His Son. The longing that Jesus showed me was in His heart for my people and was incompatible with the hatred espoused in His name.

Less than a year later, I walked down the aisle of my university's chapel to fully surrender my life to Christ.

The Decision

Then the king ordered Ashpenaz, chief of his court officials, to bring in some of the Israelites from the royal family and nobility—young men without any physical defect, handsome, showing aptitude for every kind of learning, well informed, quick to understand, and qualified to serve in the king's palace.

—DANIEL 1:3–4

We have been in Babylon for weeks now. The government has decreed that the children of the slain nobility will be inspected and interviewed. They will choose from among us. They will select the strongest and the brightest of us to study their literature and culture before becoming members of the king's court.

Before the monster executed my mother, she had seen the hate growing in my eyes. She had reminded me of Job 2:10. "'Shall we accept good from God, and not trouble,'" she had quoted to me, "when our sins are many, Daniel?"

I had never known Ma to sin. But then I realized that was the point. Even the righteous are "works in progress." When God chooses to bring us through the fire, flood waters or storm, it doesn't mean He has abandoned us. His aim is only to perfect us—no matter what it takes!

So, if I fight the Babylonians, I may be fighting God who gave us into their hands. If I hate the people the Lord sent to punish us, do I then hate His justice? I must trust in God and learn the meaning of the saying, "Though he slay me, yet will I hope in him" (Job 13:15).

A Different Kind of Man

If the king's officials select me, then I will be made a eunuch. The "I need to catch my breath" feeling that runs through me when I wait in the wake of a particular young lady to smell the perfume of her robes will vanish. She need not blush with that half smile if she catches my eye, for I will never take her as my bride. I am like a bee without a sting, wine without joy. "Though he slay me, yet will I hope in him," returns to my mind.

Moses declared in the Torah, "No one who has been emasculated by crushing or cutting may enter the assembly of the Lord" (Deut. 23:1).

As a eunuch, I will be an outcast, unable to worship in the community. My father was moved by the hand of God when he gave me the name Daniel, which means "God is my judge." Oh, how God has judged me!

The soldiers came for me. They grabbed me roughly, pulling me to my feet. They looked at each other with a smirk and brought me to the priest. A stick was placed between my teeth. My robe was opened, and it was over in a matter of minutes.

I could not walk. The slaves allowed me to put my arms around them, and they escorted me back to my room. Everything was spinning. The other boys are groaning. I will lie still until I sleep.

When Will I Awake?

I can't sleep. My fellow students call me a cult leader and a devil. The university says I am no longer welcome to be enrolled. My friends and family think I have become an extremist. Theologians have denounced me, and a number of churches in the District of Columbia have repudiated me. Why? A few weeks ago, I posted a flier that would forever change my life.

I am twenty-five years old, and it has been only five years since I walked down the aisle of the Howard University chapel to give my life to Christ. I have become the lead spokesman of the campus ministry at which I surrendered to Christ. Our group has grown from thirty to just under 200 in about a year's time.

I was preparing to teach a series that would speak from my background as someone who had considered becoming a black Muslim. I was going to dare to refute the Nation of Islam's teaching that black people are gods and white people are devils.

The flier was designed to capture the reader's attention. It showed a picture of a sign with "Beware of Dogs" written on it and the Scripture reference Philippians 3:2. At the bottom I reversed a Nation of Islam slogan by stating, "Mohammed is dead, and Allah is not God."

Sharp rhetoric was in those days the norm at my university. When I was younger, the leader of the Nation of Islam visited the campus and, with thousands of people present, suggested that the guns of black soldiers in the U.S. Army might one day be turned on former slaveholders. We gave him thunderous applause.

My flier was not aimed at orthodox Muslims, though they also took offense. I thought this was outrageous—considering that their own Quran goes much further than my gentle name-calling by commanding its adherents to kill people of different religions wherever they can be found.

The campus went into an uproar. My meetings were shut down. The university stated that they were getting calls from the Middle East and receiving bomb threats. This was a little hard for me to believe. I was young and inexperienced, and I had some important lessons to learn.

The clamor was due to the fact that I used the term "dog" to describe the opponents of the gospel. They argued that a real Christian would not use such language.

Did they not read that even our meek and lowly Jesus called a woman a dog to get her attention? (See Matthew 15:26.) Or had they never read that regarding those who opposed the gospel, the apostle Paul stated: "Watch out for those dogs, those men who do evil, those mutilators of the flesh" (Phil. 3:2).

Maybe my statement wasn't polite, but it was right. I thought it was funny that those who opposed me for using such terminology called me things a hundred times more insulting. Certainly we should be careful using such terms, but the university's reaction was overblown and unbalanced.

In New Testament times, a group called the Judaizers taught that Gentiles needed to be circumcised before they could be true Christians. Philippians 3:2 was written to address the erroneous idea that a relationship with God could be established on contrived physical distinctions.

Likewise, in the mid-1980s, members of the Nation of Islam preached that white people were devils and black people were gods. I would have had to deny the authority of the Scriptures to say my flier was wrong.

We must beware of stray dogs and the doctrines that demons teach. We should always aim to be wise and considerate, but we must not lose our sense of indignation over evil.

I was only five courses away from receiving my degree, but I was no longer welcome at my beloved university. They could have told me to improve my manners or to use more discretion in my advertising, but instead I was ruined. My name became a byword among nominal Christians and unbelievers alike.

Shortly afterward, the university seminary began to train Islamic clerics. The little chapel was turned into a mosque.

In the meantime, the controversy surrounding me caused my ministry to dwindle from a couple hundred to about thirty. My experience was prophetic—a tremendous shift was taking place in the African American community, and it was only a short time later that Nation of Islam leader Louis Farrakhan convened one million men on the Mall in Washington, D.C.

I was both isolated and demoralized. From that time on I read mostly reference books and classic Christian books to try to escape any impulse toward radical Christianity. However, the more I read the more I was forced to face the reality that the historic leaders of the Christian church were far more radical and complicated than I could ever hope to be.

During my undergraduate studies, I read about Nat Turner, Frederick Douglass, Sojourner Truth, Harriet Tubman, Booker T. Washington, Marcus Garvey, Richard Allen and, of course, Martin Luther King Jr. I found that there was little difference between them and the Augustines, Tyndales, Luthers, Calvins and Wesleys. It was becoming

undeniable to me that controversy attended all genuine spiritual leaders.

In spite of such a cloud of so many witnesses, I
began to doubt myself and my God. I began to
overly negotiate my preaching. In short, I began to
compromise.

I held a strong evangelical faith, but not in public.
Not that I stopped telling the truth—I just did not
tell the whole truth. I would speak of heaven but not
talk about hell. I would talk about truth but never
call untruth a lie. I would speak of the doves but
never mention the dogs.

Daniel and I, both eloquent but obsequious, had
a lot in common. We both sat emasculated by the
tyranny of Babylon.

Conscience

Daniel arrives in Babylon. With his new
home will come his new name and, in the
years to come, a new identity through which
God will glorify Himself.

The long journey from Israel had taken its toll on us.
By the time we arrived in Babylon, our eyes bulged like
tiny white snowballs dotted by pieces of coal. Our skin
looked like leather stretched over brittle skeletons.

To my surprise, Nebuchadnezzar was not as much
of a brute as I had expected. A quick assessor of
human nature and a natural leader, the king had
decided that instead of annihilating us he would

assimilate us into his own culture.

He picked the best-looking, smartest, strongest and most physically fit among us to receive Babylonian citizenship. The name Belteshazzar was given to me to reflect my identity as a new son of the empire. It means "may the god of Babylon protect my life."

The dark clouds that once churned violently inside me have started to roll back from my life. Color is starting to splash upon the drab recesses of my soul. My mind is clear and focused. But if I sit alone too long, I start to remember. I keep busy.

The boys and I have started to laugh again. Meshach, Shadrach and Abednego sneaked into my room and put butter on my hand while I was sleeping. They tickled my face with a leaf, and as I reached to scratch it, I smeared butter all over my face. We laughed for hours. I guess mischief is our way of quietly regaining a sense of control over our lives.

As the dinner hour approached, we could hear servants banging the silverware as they prepared the tables. A few of us dared to peek our heads into the dining room, hoping to get a whiff of the cuisine. To my surprise, the porters were lighting incense and offering the meat to their gods. Such food is unlawful for a Jew to eat.

We must have startled the servants because when they turned to look in our direction, a porter slipped and a knife being used to carve the meat for the offering flew out of his hand into the air. It was coming in my direction, so I ducked my head behind the wall. When I looked again it was landing just in front of my foot.

It bounced from tip to handle for several seconds. I went to reach for it and return it to the porter. Then very strangely, it stilled and stood like a coin on edge, with its sharp tip pointing toward the ceiling.

When I looked at it, chills ran up my spine and a pain seared through my groin. It was a phantom pain, triggered by the sight of a knife that looked exactly like the one used to cut me weeks before. The blood, the taste of the wood, the smell of flesh—it all came rushing back to my mind.

In plain view of everyone in the room, I stood frozen. In the flash of the moment it occurred to me, it is not really the physical emasculation from crushing or cutting that prohibits men from the assembly of the Lord. It is an impotence of the heart!

I turned and left the room as quietly as I had entered. I vowed not to eat the king's food.

Bon Appétit

But Daniel resolved not to defile himself with the royal food and wine, and he asked the chief official for permission not to defile himself this way. Now God had caused the official to show favor and sympathy to Daniel, but the official told Daniel, "I am afraid of my lord the king, who has assigned your food and drink. Why should he see you looking worse than the other young men your age? The king would then have my head because of you."

Daniel then said to the guard whom the chief official had appointed over Daniel, Hananiah, Mishael and Azariah, "Please test your servants for ten days: Give us nothing but vegetables to eat and water to drink. Then compare our appearance with that of the young men who eat the royal food, and treat your servants in accordance with what you see." So he agreed to this and tested them for ten days.

At the end of ten days they looked healthier and better nourished than any of the young men who ate the royal food. So the guard took away their choice food and the wine they were to drink and gave them vegetables instead.

—DANIEL 1:8–16

We were tested for ten days. We showed no improvement at first. About midway through, others thought that some of us were ill. It wasn't until the end of those days of testing that our skin had begun to shine and God had fattened our bones.

Daniel was tested for ten days, but the young college student was tested for more than ten years. However, in time he will find the verse to be true, "He who has called us is faithful." (See 1 Thessalonians 5:24.) Our faith may cost us everything. But compromise could cost us our very souls. That's a greater price than anyone should be willing to pay.

CHAPTER 2

DANIEL AND THE DREAM

In the second year of his reign, Nebuchadnezzar had dreams; his mind was troubled and he could not sleep. So the king summoned the magicians, enchanters, sorcerers and astrologers to tell him what he had dreamed. When they came in and stood before the king, he said to them, "I have had a dream that troubles me and I want to know what it means."

Then the astrologers answered the king in Aramaic, "O king, live forever! Tell your servants the dream, and we will interpret it."

The king replied to the astrologers, "This is what I have firmly decided: If you do not tell me what my dream was and interpret it, I will have you cut into pieces and your houses

turned into piles of rubble. But if you tell me
the dream and explain it, you will receive
from me gifts and rewards and great honor.
So tell me the dream and interpret it for me."
—DANIEL 2:1–6

For days the king has been irritable. Everyone in
the palace is walking on eggshells. He and his great
armies have conquered the world, but he cannot
master his own bed. He had a dream that woke him,
and his eyes have found no sleep since. Some are saying that devils are haunting the royal palace. Others
believe the gods are punishing him for his many sins.

He has called the ecumenical council of
enchanters, conjurers, fortunetellers and astrologers.
They offer no answers, only excuses. The king has
ordered the execution of all the wise men of Babylon.

We were not invited to the council. Our opinion is
not sought in the affairs of state. The Babylonians
believe their god has defeated the God of Moses. They
view warring armies as a battle between gods, not mortals. To the victor go the spoils. The Egyptians who
pursued my countrymen years ago may have been
swallowed by the Red Sea, but today the Babylonians
think one greater than any pharaoh is enthroned in the
famous Hanging Gardens of Babylon.

A New Dream

We have just shut the doors of our church in
Washington. I have told every member to find a new

church to attend. Like King Nebuchadnezzar, I keep having a dream, but when I awake it seems more like a nightmare. I know that the Lord has called me, but it does not seem that I have what it takes to be successful. I am becoming impatient with religious clichés. I have some real problems and need some solid answers. If I am not going to be more fruitful in ministry, why should I even waste my time?

I hope old Ms. Jackson finds a church where someone will pick her up every Sunday for service. She has a hard time getting around, even with her walker. I wonder how much longer Jamal is going to live and if his family will still ask me to do his funeral.

I hope Jerry stays away from the alcohol; recent problems at home seem to be pushing him over the edge. Pooky the crack dealer and I have established a rapport. His whole crew moves out of the way when I walk by. I had hoped that God would use me to reach them.

Several of my members are convinced that I am making a mistake by leaving the pastorate. For all their faults, they usually know the voice of God. My father has always criticized me for not being a finisher. But I just do not think I have the emotional or financial resources to continue.

"OK, I tell you guys what," I said to my congregants in the hope of buying some time. "We will meet on Sundays in Brother and Sister Jackson's apartment until we know for sure what to do."

Weeks turned into months. Months became almost a year. I started to dabble in another career, but the call on my life was absolutely inescapable. It whispered to me in the morning. It spoke to me over lunch and shouted at me through the night.

The great preacher Charles Spurgeon once commented, "If you can do anything else in life and be happy, you're not truly called." How right he was! A fire burned in my soul that I did not start and could not put out.

My physical problems were escalating. I was dealing with constant infections, and my bleeding was regularly staining my clothes. The pain made it difficult for me to do most things, but I was able to stand on my feet for about two hours at a time without grimacing. I was in a pretty wretched condition, but I believed that those who did not know Christ at all were still worse off than I was. I decided to return to my post and man my pulpit once again.

My preaching style had changed dramatically from my early years. I had become very theologically intentional and precise. Following in the footsteps of Martin Luther King Jr., I had begun to read Karl Barth, and he had deeply challenged my evangelical roots.

I refused to compromise my fundamental beliefs, but survival in ministry had become my major consideration. I practiced what I once was told, "If you preach to the hurts of people, you will always have a crowd."

I also avoided any public demonstration of my earlier charismatic influences. I reasoned that my critics had been right all along. I needed to tone it down and exhibit more "wisdom."

I decided not to make public prophetic utterances. I did not pray for the sick. I preached as if what was humanly reasonable was the extent of God's supernatural power. Radical faith gave way to careful planning. Team-building became more important than prayer.

We leased a local high school. About ten people attended our first service. By the end of the year we had about thirty. By the end of second year we had grown to about one hundred. I was finally fitting in. People were accepting me. We were on the road to success.

Everyone was excited, but my smile could not hide my shame. I had betrayed my Jesus.

The Last Becomes First

> When Arioch, the commander of the king's guard, had gone out to put to death the wise men of Babylon, Daniel spoke to him with wisdom and tact. He asked the king's officer, "Why did the king issue such a harsh decree?" Arioch then explained the matter to Daniel. At this, Daniel went into the king and asked for time, so that he might interpret the dream for him.
>
> —DANIEL 2:14–16

I was surprised when the king's royal guard pounded on my front door. It was early in the morning, and I had just finished my time of prayer. The other wise men typically ridiculed me, but the soldiers had taken a liking to me. They spoke to me so formally that I knew something was terribly wrong.

I asked the king's officer why they had come. The guards grabbed my arms as they had done once before. The officer explained the situation. He stated that I would have to be put to death. Upon hearing this, I asked to be taken to the king to interpret his dream. The officer was reluctant, but out of kindness toward me, he got the approval.

On the way to the palace, I saw all the other wise men assembled in the court. When I walked past them our garments were taken by the wind. I pushed my fluttering headpiece from my face and turned to look the men in the eye.

No one uttered a word. It was surreal. The breeze cooled us, but our garments whipped like flags at half-staff, their flapping sounding a death knoll that only the initiated could hear.

I turned away to look in the direction of the throne room. How different it was this day. The grounds that were so often abuzz with the activity of the king's worshipers had been struck by an uneasy silence.

On a normal day, one group would dissect the dung of the king for omens. Another would stare off into the night sky to chart the stars. After high ceremonies, a priest would invariably fall to the floor kicking and flailing his arms in a trance-like state, channeling messages from the world beyond.

Today they all have nothing to say. No omen. No utterance. No hope.

I suppose Meshach, Shadrach, Abednego and I seem as strange to them as they do to us. We bob back and forth in reverence when we read the Torah, uttering it aloud just above our breath. Every day we recite, "Hear, O Israel: The LORD our God, the LORD is one" (Deut. 6:4). They think we are unsophisticated for not bowing to their gods. This is a major point of contention between us and them.

The king extended his scepter to me and allowed me to speak. He had bags under his eyes. He sat on his throne leaning his head on his right elbow. He seemed relieved to have me approach, and sat up.

I asked him to allow me time to seek the God of Abraham, Isaac and Jacob for an answer to his request. He looked at me impatiently, then paused and waved his arm in the air to indicate that he wanted me to leave his presence. I was not clear if he was granting my request or declining it.

The Dream

> Then Daniel returned to his house and explained the matter to his friends Hananiah, Mishael and Azariah. He urged them to plead for mercy from the God of heaven concerning this mystery, so that he and his friends might not be executed with the rest of the wise men of Babylon. During the night the mystery was revealed to Daniel in a vision. Then Daniel praised the God of heaven.
>
> —DANIEL 2:17–19

I know a lot about what the king was experiencing. After the death of my parents, I too was haunted by nightmares. Sometimes I was even afraid to sleep. God delivered me, and He will deliver the king.

The day was long. I was tired by the time I returned home. Already the shadows of evening are dancing upon my walls. Will the king have patience? I prostrated myself before my God and opened my heart to His voice. I asked God to give me the king's vision.

God answered, and I saw things too great for a man to see. I saw the future and He who holds it, the three empires that would follow Babylon, and even a glimpse into an eternal kingdom. The king agreed to see me again.

"The vision was so clear, Your Majesty," I said to him. "In it I saw a statue of a man. The head of the statue was made of gold, which represented Babylon. The chest and arms were crafted of silver, the belly and thighs of bronze. The legs were made of iron and the feet of iron mixed with clay.

"The values of the metals decreased from head to foot, which reflected the increasing weakness in the forms of government that will follow you, great Nebuchadnezzar. On the other hand, Your Majesty, the strength of the metals increased from top to bottom. This indicates the increasing endurance and longevity of each successive empire."

The king was astounded by my dream and interpretation:

> Then King Nebuchadnezzar fell prostrate before Daniel and paid him honor and ordered that an offering and incense be presented to him. The king said to Daniel,

"Surely your God is the God of gods and the Lord of kings and a revealer of mysteries, for you were able to reveal this mystery."

Then the king placed Daniel in a high position and lavished many gifts on him. He made him ruler over the entire province of Babylon and placed him in charge of all its wise men. Moreover, at Daniel's request the king appointed Shadrach, Meshach and Abednego administrators over the province of Babylon, while Daniel himself remained at the royal court.

—DANIEL 2:46–49

While Daniel stayed awake to interpret the king's dream, a weariness of soul overcomes our other young man, and he begins to sleep on the job.

A Moment of Clarity

The ministry was growing, but it still had more than $40,000 of debt that I personally secured. During this time, my wife bore our second son.

Our Sunday offerings were low but increasing. I took home less than a third of my salary that year. We lived in one of the most expensive counties in the United States but I earned below the national poverty line. I had no disability insurance.

I had undergone a third surgery, but it too was unsuccessful. The pilonidal cyst was about seven inches long and three inches wide. At this point my body was always bloody, and I was in too much pain to consider getting another professional job.

Soon the church was collecting a few thousand dollars a month. I appointed new leaders to the church board. They took their jobs seriously. In fact, most of them believed they should run the church.

After two years of my hard work, the church was in a position to support me financially. Yet I was told to get a second job. I had spent hours a day in my weakened condition walking the neighborhood handing out thousands of fliers a month in addition to the more than forty hours a week I had given to meeting the needs of my congregation.

For this the Bible states a commandment as sure as any other God ever made, "In the same way, the Lord has commanded that those who preach the gospel should receive their living from the gospel" (1 Cor. 9:14). Due to Paul's traveling ministry and the appearance of impropriety that might follow him if he practiced receiving money from a church in one city and then moving to the next, God gave him the only exception recorded in Scripture. That passage also meant that Paul forfeited the right to be married to fulfill his ministry.

I had no such ministry and two young children who needed Dad to have some time for them. What might it profit a pastor to gain a large church but lose his own sons? I was not functioning in an apostolic ministry such as Paul's. I was merely a pastor, and our church was to function under biblical mandate.

In spite of my chronic illness, I was in the homes

of my church members fixing toilets, giving rides and sharing dinners. I was counseling, praying, studying, coordinating and managing the business affairs of the church. At night I would lay my head on my pillow only to be awakened by phone calls. I thought that if my congregation placed so little value in my life and service, something had gone very wrong.

Finally, I got up one morning and looked at myself in the mirror, realizing I had become everything I despised. I had become a lackey, a religious whipping boy for miserable people. I looked at my two boys and thought, please don't grow up and be like me.

I shook my head, refusing to let this go on any longer. In that moment I felt my strength return—like Sampson who stood shackled in bronze and his eyes gouged out in disgrace, God was at work behind the scenes and caused his hair to grow back. Not unlike this fallen hero, I stood between my two pillars of compromise and self-doubt and began to push. I said the word that has changed my life— "No!" (See Judges 16:22.)

I stopped trying to be the mild-mannered, likeable pastor. Once again I endeavored to be a man of God.

The household income of many of my members is more than $100,000 per year. Why should my congregation's wives and children be more important than my own? Am I less than these other men, simply because I am a preacher? Is this really God's plan for church life?

By this time the church owed me more than $20,000 in back salary. If the church folded, I would also be personally responsible for more than $40,000 of debt. I decided to take charge of my situation and told the secretary and treasurer to write me a minimal check for $500, which was well within my rights as the organization's president.

The chairman of the board called me and told me that I should not do it. He gave no reason. He just told me that he did not "feel" that the church should do it, even though being paid by the church was part of my salary agreement.

Of course, the $500 did little to help financially. The principle of the matter was what was important. I wasn't less than a man because I was a preacher, and I shouldn't have to live as if I were. If I worked, I should be compensated.

I decided that if God had called me to lead a church, then I must be a leader. I knew that I would pay dearly for my decision. But I knew that even though I could lose this church and have to spend the next twenty years paying this debt myself, I would be respected.

I refused to compromise anymore. I would preach the gospel without compromise and God could either keep me or let me fall. If I fell, then I'd know my gospel wasn't true.

I realized that what I compromised in order to keep I would lose anyway. I had two sons to raise and a wife to care for, and I would do it with honor!

CHAPTER 3

DANIEL AND THE MADMAN

I, Nebuchadnezzar, was at home in my palace, contented and prosperous.

—DANIEL 4:4

Seafarers warn their apprentices that calm seas are the most dangerous kind. The bright skies and gentle rocking motion of the waves can lull a sailor into a false sense of security. He may grow unconcerned about holding on to the rails as he walks about the boat, or clinging tightly to something stable when he is climbing the mast.

Storms at sea often occur suddenly. Their unpredictability can have deadly consequences. One moment the crew is whistling in the sunlight. The next, fifteen-foot waves are nearly dashing the ship. I think the writer of the letters to the Corinthian

church—the apostle Paul—had his many experiences
on the high seas in mind when he wrote, "So, if you
think you are standing firm, be careful that you don't
fall!" (1 Cor. 10:12).

My name is Yeromitou. I am a native of Ethiopia.
I fell in love with an African American pastor in
1993. He told me of his struggles as a pastor over
the years, but he carried it so well that it really did
not matter to me. We met in May and were married
nine months later.

I was raised in the Orthodox Church. In my country our priests and mother church were treated with
great respect and love, but in the United States it is
very different.

It was not long before I realized that when you
marry a pastor, you also marry his church. This was
the most difficult part of my husband's and my relationship. After two years of bringing my newborn
baby into dangerous drug-infested streets and a rat-
infested church building, I was relieved when the
church shut down. I hurt for my husband, but all
that little church did was drain our resources and
energy—from the very first night we were there
when two men tried to steal my purse.

Things were financially tight for us at times, but
my husband always provided for us in the long run.
It was not the financial issues alone that made me
want my husband to do more with his life; it was also
the ingratitude and constant bickering in the church.

When things were hard for us, it was natural for
me to be skeptical and keep a healthy distance from

our church members. But when we moved the church to Virginia, the congregation doubled the first year. It tripled the second year, and for the first time people seemed interested in helping my husband fulfill his vision.

My husband and I grew very close to our congregants. We loved them, not only in the pastoral sense, but also as friends, even as family. We felt secure. We trusted in men—and would soon pay the price for that.

As time went on, my husband started to feel uneasy and called for an all-night prayer meeting. During our gathering he preached about Korah and Moses. He spoke as if God were speaking through him, something he had not done for a long time.

Near the end of the meeting, everyone heard knocking at the front door. Three times we went to the door, but nobody was there. Then my husband quoted John the disciple's words of Jesus, "'Here I am! I stand at the door and knock'" (Rev. 3:20). It was a little scary.

Within two weeks of our prayer meeting, people who we thought were our dearest friends had turned on us and become enemies. Without knowing it, we had become puppets, constantly trying to satisfy the desires of others. The time had come to cut the strings.

My husband took a stand against a board member over a trivial matter and finally said no to this man, and refused to change his mind. He went to lunch with the gentleman and grew even stronger. Derek told him that if he could not accept his leadership in areas that Derek had responsibility for, then the man would have to find another pastor. Hell broke loose— a reminder of Paul's warning: "So, if you think you are standing firm, be careful that you don't fall!"

Homecoming

Daniel leaves Babylon and returns to find a very different king.

I have been out of Babylon for several months. While I was gone, the dream God gave Nebuchadnezzar really went to his head. The king commanded that the statue he saw in his dream be crafted for him. It is nine feet wide and ninety feet high and plated in pure gold. Because he left out all the other metals, it is clear that he has revised my interpretation of the dream and thinks Babylon will be an everlasting kingdom.

When he held the public dedication of the statue, he demanded that all of his officials and servants bow and worship the image. My friends Shadrach, Meshach and Abednego refused and were cast into the fiery furnace. God miraculously intervened and saved their lives, but all is still not well in the kingdom.

Nebuchadnezzar has dreamed another dream. But it's as if he still doesn't understand. The Most High God caused me to dream his dream and then inter-pret it. Nebuchadnezzar even saw the Son of Man walking unharmed in the fire while he was trying to burn my three friends. But still he calls for magicians, enchanters, astrologers and diviners before he calls for the servants of the Most High God.

I will report the rest of the story from the king's own annals:

I said, "Belteshazzar, chief of the magicians, I know the spirit of the holy gods is in you...Here is my dream, interpret it for me." Then Daniel (also called Belteshazzar) was greatly perplexed for a time, and his thoughts terrified him. So the king said, "Belteshazzar, do not let the dream or its meaning alarm you."

Belteshazzar answered, "My lord, if only the dream applied to your enemies and its meaning to your adversaries!...You, O king, saw a messenger, a holy one, coming down from heaven and saying, 'Cut down the tree and destroy it, but leave the stump, bound with iron and bronze, in the grass of the field, while its roots remain in the ground. Let him be drenched with the dew of heaven; let him live like the wild animals, until seven times pass by for him.'

"You will be driven away from people and will live with the wild animals; you will eat grass like cattle and be drenched with the dew of heaven. Seven times will pass by for you until you acknowledge that the Most High is sovereign over the kingdoms of men and gives them to anyone he wishes."

—DANIEL 4:9, 19, 23, 25

> The command to leave the stump of the tree with its roots means that your kingdom will be restored to you when you acknowledge God rules. Therefore, O king, please accept my advice: Renounce your sins by doing what is right, and your wickedness to being kind to the oppressed. It may be that your prosperity will continue.

Nebuchadnezzar refused to heed God's warning. Twelve months after I interpreted the dream, the king was walking on the roof of his palace. He had become so impressed with his hanging gardens and his great armies.

In the distance he could see his many fields of bounty. Servants catered to his every whim, and princes were forced to hang upon his every word. In his own eyes he had become more than a king; he had become a god. Caught up in what he perceived as his own greatness, he spoke aloud as if the one true God had no ears.

> "Is not this the great Babylon I have built as the royal residence, by my mighty power and for the glory of my majesty?"
>
> —Daniel 4:30

While the words were still on his lips, the king who believed he was a god lost the faculties that made him even a man. From that moment on, he became like a beast and began to eat grass like cattle and roam the outdoors like any animal of the field. His body hair was soon matted like the feathers of a bird. His nails grew so long they curled and turned brown. The king had gone mad and so had his kingdom.

Madness

It has been hard to get out of bed in the morning. My husband wakes up at night speaking in tongues. Sometimes he wakes up quoting scriptures. Other times he wakes up and just says that he is going to win, as if someone is really listening.

I know he is afraid, but he will not show it. My heart hurts in places I did not know existed. The angry board members have contacted all our leaders and accused us of things too awful to tell. They have told us they will pool their resources to destroy us. They are even prophesying these things in the name of the Lord.

The church shrinks every week. We have more than $40,000 in ministry debt that is secured by us. Our church has become too small to pay salaries. My husband is constantly bleeding from his wound, which I clean every night. It stays inflamed. We have no disability insurance.

He has started to vomit at night. I usually vomit in the mornings. Is this the life God wants for my two boys? My only comfort is that they are too young to understand what is happening.

Today I took the boys to the local library to read to them. First I stopped at the recreation center across the street to sign up for an aerobics class. There I saw the wife of a board member who was behind many of the problems that her husband was creating for Derek.

The moment she saw me, she started yelling and calling me names while following me around the building. I tried to stay calm and to talk to her. She seemed like she was out of her mind. When she approached me closely, my kids started to cry. Still, she kept hollering.

I clutched my one child in my arm, and pushed my youngest in his stroller toward the door. This woman wasn't going to give up that easily. She followed me to the parking lot and didn't leave until I reached the door of my car.

I was both angry and afraid. I couldn't stop shaking. Now my children had been brought into the madness. When I got home I told my husband what had happened. We immediately called the police. They told us that there was nothing they could do.

Because there were so many church members like this, and because we didn't know when or where we might encounter them, there were days when I did not want to leave my house. Wherever we went we had to look over our shoulders. We had become like prisoners in our own town.

Soon after this, the worship leader and the woman who had followed me through the rec center started a telephone campaign against us. Then the head usher and his family and friends left the church. More and more people stopped coming to church. Every Sunday we had to drag ourselves to service. It had started to feel more like a funeral than a celebration of life.

Over the next six months, our membership dropped from 100 people to about thirty. As a church, we were finished. It would take years for Derek to pay off the debts, but he refused to declare bankruptcy.

I asked him one night why he was torturing himself and us by staying in the ministry. I told him to quit for our children's sake. Our people, like King Nebuchadnezzar, had started to act like animals—and I wanted out.

It was at this time that my husband began to preach with a boldness I had never seen in him before. He would say things from the pulpit like, "God would have to self-destruct and be found a liar before I would fail." He believed that strongly in God's promises. I didn't understand his newfound confidence.

But like the stump in Nebuchadnezzar's dream that was bound with iron and brass while its root remained in the ground, our church began suddenly to grow like it had never grown before. In less than six months we had added another 100 people. This time, however, it happened without "people-pleasing" on our part. Derek preached the unadulterated Word of God. That was his only intention.

At the time it seemed as if my family would be indebted for the next twenty years from the church expenses we had incurred; yet, within a year and a half from the church split all our debts were paid in full. The members of our church also began to prosper both financially and relationally. Our services had become filled with joy and excitement.

Only weeks after my husband had started to preach strongly he was scheduled to undergo surgery for a fourth time. He had suffered many years with his wound, and once again medical intervention was needed.

About seven days before the scheduled surgery, his doctor had inspected his wound, expecting within a week to be operating on it. But by the end of the week my husband had called for an emergency appointment with his doctor. Something had happened to the affected area—the wound was completely closed.

After years of chronic pain, infection and bleeding, he had been miraculously healed. After inspecting my husband, his physician cancelled the surgery. My husband and I vowed to never compromise again.

Just a few months later, in his mid-thirties, my husband turned his negative energies into work and went back to school to earn a master's degree. By age thirty-six, he had also completed his doctorate. The church continued to grow, and my husband finally was compensated financially. That same year, we sold our townhome and still had more than $100,000 after we had given away gifts and loans. With the money we created a nest egg and purchased a beautiful new home. God is faithful.

> At the end of that time, I, Nebuchadnezzar, raised my eyes toward heaven, and my sanity was restored. Then I praised the Most High; I honored and glorified him who lives forever.
>
> At the same time that my sanity was

restored, my honor and splendor were returned to me for the glory of my kingdom. My advisers and nobles sought me out, and I was restored to my throne and became even greater than before. Now I, Nebuchadnezzar, praise and exalt and glorify the King of heaven, because everything he does is right and all his ways are just. And those who walk in pride he is able to humble.

—DANIEL 4:34, 36–37

When Nebuchadnezzar looked to the heavens, God restored his sanity. If we would look again toward heaven and re-establish the kingdom of Christ as our ultimate priority, we would find that God has a way of restoring all we have lost. Just as God said to a people who seemed to be without hope, so He says to us:

"I will repay you for the years the locusts have eaten—the great locust and the young locust, the other locusts and locust swarm— my great army that I sent among you. You will have plenty to eat, until you are full, and you will praise the name of the Lord your God, who has worked wonders for you; never again will my people be shamed."

—JOEL 2:25–26

CHAPTER 4

DANIEL AND THE WRITING ON THE WALL

Nebuchadnezzar is finally gone. The great king has gone the way of all mortals. Funeral pyres are lit throughout the hill country. We have buried a giant—and with him the glory of Babylon. The kingdom has lost its compass, and the empire is plunging into turmoil.

Our monarchy has been beset with intrigue and violence. Belshazzar, Nebuchadnezzar's son, will rule. He is a soft man, given to pleasure and pretense. He is a descendant of Nebuchadnezzar, but in name and bloodline only. When the Persians attacked Babylon, Belshazzar stayed at home in the palace, drinking wine and engaging in things unspeakable.

At every turn he attempts to outdo his own

debauchery. He has become more and more out-landish. He and all the princes are familiar with the stories of his father and the God of Daniel. But the prince has gone beyond restraint.

> While Belshazzar was drinking his wine, he gave orders to bring in the gold and silver goblets that Nebuchadnezzar his father had taken from the temple in Jerusalem, so that the king and his nobles, his wives and his concubines might drink from them. As they drank the wine they praised the gods of gold and silver, of bronze, iron, wood and stone.
>
> —DANIEL 5:2, 4

> He called for goblets of the temple of Jerusalem and toasted the gods of gold and silver. He was very satisfied with his perfor-mance. However, not only did the dinner-ware belong to God, but also his empire.
>
> Suddenly the fingers of a human hand appeared and wrote on the plaster of the wall, near the lampstand in the royal palace. The king watched the hand as it wrote.
>
> —DANIEL 5:5

The guards extended their swords and rushed toward the spectacle, expecting to see the face of the uninvited guest. The servants were commanded to bring their torches, but natural light could not illu-mine the identity of the writer. No face, no body—only the strong and thick fingers of a man who seemed to hold the strength of the universe in them.

A Little Knee-Knocking

> His face turned pale and he was so frightened that his knees knocked together and his legs gave way.
>
> —DANIEL 5:6

Belshazzar was frightened beyond words. His bony, naked knees knocked. His skin grew pale, and forgetting all royal dignity, he fell to the floor, exhaling a high pitched, *Uhhh!* When the guests and onlookers saw the prince's body hit the ground, they held their hands to their mouths. Pandemonium set in.

> The king called out for the enchanters, astrologers, and diviners to be brought... Then all the king's wise men came in, but they could not read the writing or tell the king what it meant. So King Belshazzar became even more terrified and his face grew more pale. His nobles were baffled.
>
> —DANIEL 5:7–9

By this time the prancing about of dignitaries and the tumult of the crowd had caught the ear of Nitocris—Belshazzar's mother and the widow of Nebuchadnezzar. Now aged and much more fragile than in her full-bodied youth, she entered the throne room. Two maids attended to her, helping her support herself.

> "O king, live forever!" she said. "Don't be alarmed! Don't look so pale! There is a man

in your kingdom who has the spirit of the
holy gods in him…Your father—your father
the king, I say—appointed him chief of the
magicians, enchanters, astrologers and diviners. This man Daniel, whom the king called
Belteshazzar, was found to have a keen mind
and knowledge and understanding, and also
the ability to interpret dreams, explain rid-
dles and solve difficult problems. Call for
Daniel and he will tell you what the writing
means."

—DANIEL 5:10–12

Test of Faith

The handwriting was on the wall for
another young man. Unless he takes up the
cross and embraces the sometimes rough
message of the gospel he too will be
weighed in the balance.

About one year after my conversion, Jesus
appeared to me a second time. It was a typical
Wednesday evening, and I was preparing to attend
mid-week services at my church. I almost never
missed a service, but I felt strongly that I should not
attend that night.

My girlfriend at that time went on to the service
and left me alone in her apartment. Only moments
after she left, I sensed the presence of God in the
room. It seemed to emanate from behind me.
Turning to look, I saw Jesus hanging on the cross. A

new reverence for Him immediately was burned deep into my spirit.

The agony of Christ is usually what is depicted when we view artistic depictions of Calvary. In the vision I had of Him, His suffering was very clear, but it was not the major emphasis being conveyed.

His character and the depth of His soul eclipsed the gruesomeness of it all. He was not just another criminal hanging on a cross. He was God speaking from eternity, through an illustrative sermon that was so much larger than my feeling. All I could do was weep with a deep, guttural type of moan.

The feeling of His presence intensified. I felt my body tingling all over, and it was as if a blanket of peace was being wrapped all around me. Jesus then spoke to me. He said, "Stand up, close your eyes, bend over and go wherever I lead you." I leaned forward as if I were carrying a cross on my back. Luke 9:23—"'If anyone would come after Me, he must deny himself and take up his cross and follow Me'"—coursed through my mind.

He instructed me to walk quickly. I began to navigate myself around the furnished room, and I started to think about how stupid this exercise seemed. *I have really lost it!* I thought. *I'm walking around a room pretending I have a cross on my back.*

Like Peter who began walking on the water only to start sinking I allowed my lack of faith to interrupt. God sharply rebuked me. Tears of frustration welled in my eyes as I wished that I had not questioned the will of God.

Today when I think back on this event, I realize how prophetic it was. So often I would begin something for God, but when persecution or difficulties would come, I would start to severely second-guess myself. Doubt would grip my soul, and my lack of confidence would almost make me quit and turn away. That particular problem has plagued me for years.

When my girlfriend returned to the apartment, she was very excited. Her eyes were puffy, and her cheeks were red. She asked me if anything had happened in the apartment while she was gone.

"Jesus was here," I told her. She jumped up and down and told me that while she was in the service, she saw both Jesus and me and that He was standing above me.

Older Now

Daniel has aged. He is as old as the Queen Mother. He greeted the queen with a kiss but looked in Belshazzar's direction only to wave his hands to refuse his pleasantries.

"But you his son, O Belshazzar, have not humbled yourself, though you knew all this. Instead, you have set yourself up against the Lord of heaven. You had the goblets from his temple brought to you, and you and your nobles, your wives and your concubines drank wine from them.

"You praised the gods of silver and gold,

of bronze, iron, wood and stone, which cannot see or hear or understand. But you did not honor the God who holds in his hand your life and all your ways. Therefore he sent the hand that wrote the inscription.

"This is the inscription that was written: Mene, Mene, Tekel, Parsin.

This is what these words mean: Mene: God has numbered the days of your reign and brought it to an end. Tekel: You have been weighed on the scales and found wanting. Peres: Your kingdom is divided and given to the Medes and Persians."

Then at Belshazzar's command, Daniel was clothed in purple, a gold chain was placed around his neck, and he was proclaimed the third highest ruler in the kingdom.

—DANIEL 5:22–29

As he spoke, the Babylonian army was losing its last battle just outside the city gates. Belshazzar was partying with his nobles and making light of the sacred light-bearer, but Cyrus and his army had already entered the city.

Jesus tells us that it will be the same way when He returns:

"No one knows about that day or the hour, not even the angels in heaven, nor the Son, but only the Father. As it was in the days of Noah, so it will be at the coming of the Son of Man. For in the days before the flood, people were eating and drinking, marrying and giving in marriage, up to the day Noah entered the ark; and they knew nothing about what would happen until the flood came and took them away."

—MATTHEW 24:36–39

Would you be ready if Jesus returned the moment you finished reading this sentence? If you are not 100 percent sure, fall to your knees and pray with me:

Father, forgive me for all my sins. I believe that Jesus died for me and has risen from the grave for me. Holy Spirit, come into my forgiven heart. Now teach me Your ways that I may enjoy Your presence for the rest of my days. Amen.

CHAPTER 5

STILL STANDING

When the Median-Persian army approached Babylon, the people offered no resistance. They threw open the city gates and welcomed Cyrus the Great with shouts of joy. Just as it was pictured in my dream, the head of gold—the kingdom of Nebuchadnezzar—is no more. The chest and arms of silver will reign until the bronze period.

I have been in Babylon for more than seventy years. I have outlived every king. I have traveled much of the known world and have seen more than I'll ever dare tell. My knees have become callused from my long hours of prayer, spent to cleanse my soul of the pollution from living in this strange land. Yahweh has been nearer than my closest friends. Even at my advanced age I feel His strength in my body propelling me on.

My days are nearing their end. I try to spend as much time as possible with the young men, telling them of my life's lessons. They pay careful attention; still, they seem much more complacent than we were as youths.

The Boat

Both Daniel and Derek find themselves arrested—one by a mortal king; the other by the King Eternal.

In my early twenties I had a third vision. After my morning prayer, I sat down in my bedroom chair and put on some music. Suddenly, it was as if a television were turned on inside me. I stood and walked over to turn off the music. As I did, I closed and opened my eyes several times to see if the picture would go away. When I would open my eyes, I would see my natural surroundings. When I would close my eyes, I would see a scene in which the colors were more beautiful than anything I had ever witnessed.

I had never experienced anything like it. I did not know what to do, but I was too curious to ignore it. I remained standing, and I closed my eyes and got lost in the picture within. All awareness of the things around me stopped.

In the vision, I was sitting on a fishing chair in the back of a boat. I was wearing my favorite summer hat. Various groups of people, as well as a blue dog, came running up my fishing line.

The color blue, I believe, represented the grace of God. The dog represented some of my friends who were members of a fraternity I had influenced for Christ. They called themselves "Q Dogs."

As the groups came into the boat, I opened the hull, and they went in. All the people wore bright Hawaiian clothes. I think the colorful clothing represented the free-spirited college atmosphere we all lived in.

Suddenly, a blue fish jumped out of the water, swallowed me and brought me to a dock. Then I saw Jesus. He was standing behind the steering wheel of the boat from which the fish took me. He wore a blue captain's hat, and His demeanor was all business.

> For it became him, for whom are all things, and by whom are all things, in bringing many sons unto glory, to make the captain of their salvation perfect through sufferings.
> —HEBREWS 2:10, KJV

When He arrived at the dock, I paused to stare at Him. It was as if time stopped; He possessed such control. Without getting out of the boat or moving from behind the wheel, He simply said, "Let Me show you how it was supposed to happen."

Instantly, the boat was back in the middle of the water. Instead of opening the door for the people to go into the hull, as I had done before, I was in the cabin on top of the boat. This time I was tucking all my passengers into bed. Jesus said: "Come to me, all you who are weary and burdened, and I will give you rest" (Matt. 11:28).

It was becoming clear that God was asking me to do more than invite people into His kingdom. He wanted me to participate in their pastoral care.

Somehow I traveled from the inside cabin to the deck of the boat. Again, Jesus appeared. He was walking above the water. It was hard to see his features. His face seemed to be made of glory that radiated His presence.

I am sure that He had features, but I cannot describe them. His beauty was consummate, but it was not really aesthetic—like a man's or woman's face is beautiful. It was His very essence that exuded beauty.

It was like a breathtaking moment when we suddenly find ourselves face-to-face with an alligator in the wild. We are captured by his beauty but in awe of his strength, and we dare not move.

His hair was not long, and He did not appear to be much taller than six feet. His robe fit Him well. He was not fat or skinny; He just seemed perfect.

He had white feet. Later in the vision He explained His feet this way, "Up till this time, the white man has carried My gospel into the world, but this will change."

As I have already written, I was trained that Christianity was a white man's religion. After I became a Christian I faced many moments in the church when it seemed like this was true—that Christianity was a white man's religion. I think He was addressing that.

People always wonder what color Jesus is. Since He lives in us through the Holy Spirit, He is the color of whatever house He lives in. Except for His feet, He was my exact hue. He was probably my height—I am a little over six feet tall. Whether or not this is His historical color or height is really not an issue we should waste time debating.

While He was on the water, I asked him, "Lord, why did the fish swallow me up?"

He stretched out His arm, and then pointed His finger at me. He said in the sternest voice I had ever heard, "Because you did not obey My word."

I asked Him, "What word?"

He said, "Feed my fish."

He was clarifying His former command for me to feed His sheep.

Several months before this vision the Lord had said to me in a voice as clear as I have ever heard: "Simon, son of Jonas, do you love Me?" He paused, then continued, "Feed My sheep." (See John 21:15–18.)

I really did not understand what He was trying to tell me but it had a sense of destiny attached to it. I thought about it for a while but did not really plan to obey the statement. I was completing my business degree and had every intention of becoming a businessman.

In addition, I knew nothing of shepherding. The reference seemed veiled to me. I ignored it.

As a child, however, I had kept a fish tank. Every

day I would have to feed my fish. The tropical fish I owned were helpless. Without my care, they would have died.

This time, Jesus' meaning was unmistakable. He was calling me into full-time ministry.

After He told me to feed His fish, I thought, *Why didn't I do it?* I was not asking the Lord, but myself. He answered my thought and said in a piercing tone, "Because of hate, doubt and fear!"

A little smart-mouthed, I asked Him, "Who do I hate?" I thought He was going to say white people, because I kept thinking that His white feet seemed so out of place.

His response was quite the contrary.

"Yourself!" He said.

His answer reached into my heart and made me speechless. I finally understood why the disciples were at times to afraid to ask Him anything else. (See Mark 9:32.)

Suddenly, the boat I was on returned to the dock. I gave the people a hand as they stepped off the boat. Then the Lord said, "You are on the shore of the apostles and prophets." Perhaps one day I will add to my pastoral ministry and embrace higher-level assignments for the kingdom of God.

Finally, when all of my passengers left, a girl returned and put what appeared to be a lei necklace around my neck. On my neck it became a harness, or what the Bible calls a "yoke."

In the Bible, marriage is often called a yoke. My college years had been the greatest time of friendship, work and pleasure in my life. I believe the Lord was promising that He would give me a wife who would bring back the joy I once had.

After the girl walked away, the scene disappeared.

Still Standing

Now Daniel so distinguished himself among the administrators and the satraps by his exceptional qualities that the king planned to set him over the whole kingdom.

At this, the administrators and satraps tried to find grounds for charges against Daniel in his conduct of government affairs, but they were unable to do so. They could find no corruption in him, because he was trustworthy and neither corrupt nor negligent.

Finally, these men said, "We will never find any basis for charges against this man Daniel unless it has something to do with the law of his God."

So the administrators and the satraps went as a group to the king and said: "O King Darius, live forever! The royal administrators, prefects, satraps, advisers and governors have all agreed that the king should issue an edict and enforce the decree that anyone who prays to any god or man during the next thirty days, except to you, O king, shall be thrown into the lions' den."

Now when Daniel learned that the decree had been published, he went home to his

upstairs room where the windows opened
toward Jerusalem. Three times a day he…
prayed, giving thanks to his God, just as he
had done before.

—DANIEL 6:3–7, 10

Daniel's aides rushed into his hall. Their faces were
ashen. He looked up from his chair and told them to
calm themselves and tell him their hearts. They told
him the news.

Daniel paused and leaned back on his chair. He
smiled and patted each attendant on the face as he
exited the palace grounds. They wanted to go with
him, but he motioned with his hands for them to
leave him. They followed from a distance.

He took a last look at the palace and the beautiful
gardens. He remembered how by the rivers of
Babylon he had sat and wept. He remembered the
soot, the smoke, the piercing screams, the blood and
the rapes that had brought him there in the first
place.

*Grandpa, Grandma, Mom, Dad, Sister—all have
passed on. I am all that is left of my generation,* he
thought. *Yet if I forget you, O Jerusalem, may my
right hand forget its skill. May my tongue cleave to the
roof of my mouth if I do not remember you, if I do not
consider Jerusalem, my highest joy!*

Meanwhile, his aides talked amongst themselves:

"He knew he was being followed," one said. His
neighbors had paused to smile but stopped what
they were doing to watch him walk by.

"They knew him well," said another. "They knew

he had decided to do what he had always done—pray."

Another recalled: "Remember how he used to say: "My eyes have seen the glory of the coming of the Lord. He is trampling out the vintage where the grapes of wrath are stored. His truth is marching on. I may be old but I am still standing.'"

"It's not surprising," added one other, "that he went to his room and opened his windows for all to see, and he prayed."

> So they went to the king and spoke to him about his royal decree: "Did you not publish a decree that during the next thirty days anyone who prays to any god or man except to you, O king, would be put into the lions' den?"
>
> So the king gave the order, and they brought Daniel and threw him into the lions' den. The king said to Daniel, "May your God...rescue you!"
>
> A stone was brought and placed over the mouth of the den, and the king sealed it with his own signet ring and with the rings of the nobles, so that Daniel's situation might not be changed. Then the king returned to his palace and spent the night without eating and without any entertainment being brought to him. And he could not sleep.
>
> —DANIEL 6:12, 16–18

I have spent many sleepless nights smelling the breath of ferocious lions ready to make a meal of my soul. Many times I thought my war was against certain individuals and even institutions, but over time I realized that the battles and the real war were waged within.

"Lord, why did the fish swallow me up?" I asked
"Because you did not obey My word."
"Lord, who do I hate?"
"Yourself," he answered.

Like Jonah in the belly of the fish, my inner life was wrapped with the sea weeds of self-hate, persisting doubts of God's love for me and an overwhelming fear of man.

Blue is the color of grace. The blue fish was a symbol of His grace. My struggles have been some of God's greatest gifts. I have come to thank God for all those who have opposed me. They have only helped me grow. I have come face-to-face with my personal demons and have won!

I was nineteen when He appeared to me in my dorm room. I have just turned thirty-seven. My sideburns are starting to turn gray, but I have earned a right to say with King David, "I was young and now I am old, yet I have never seen the righteous forsaken or their children begging bread" (Ps. 37:25).

> At the first light of dawn, the king got up and hurried to the lions' den. When he came near the den, he called to Daniel in an anguished voice, "Daniel, servant of the living God, has your God, whom you serve continually, been able to rescue you from the lions?"

Daniel answered, "O king, live forever!"

At the king's command, the men who had falsely accused Daniel were brought in and thrown into the lions' den, along with their wives and children. And before they reached the floor of the den, the lions overpowered them and crushed all their bones.

—DANIEL 6:19–21, 24

Francis of Assisi once said, "Preach the gospel always, and if necessary, use words." Daniel was such a man; he preached with much more than words. His life has spoken volumes.

Thanks, Daniel. Our years go by quickly. I will see you soon.

ABOUT THE AUTHOR

Derek Grier, while a student at Howard University, had a supernatural encounter with Jesus. This encounter led him to give his life to the Lord. In 1989, he answered the call into the ministry and became the leader of what would become the largest campus ministry at his alma mater. He later held his first pastorate in a small storefront church among the prostitutes and homeless in a drug infested area of Washington, D.C. He often comments that this is where he really attended seminary. He has earned a M.Ed. from Regent University and a D.Min. from Wagner Leadership Institute. He is currently the founding pastor of Grace Christian Church in Woodbridge, Virginia.

Dr. Grier has served as the senior editor of *Diaspora Magazine*, a publication he founded in the mid-nineties. During its operation it was the largest Christian magazine targeted to African-American youth. He is currently serving a two-year term as co-president of the Eastern Prince William Ministerial Association, which convenes over one hundred pastors across racial and denominational lines. He is a highly regarded communicator of the gospel and has been included in *Who's Who of America* as one of our nation's outstanding Christian leaders.

Dr. Grier and his Ethiopian born wife, Yeromitou, and their two sons, Derek Jr. and David, reside in the D.C. metropolitan area.

TO CONTACT THE AUTHOR

Dr. Derek Grier
P.O. Box 5326
Woodbridge, VA 22194
E-mail: pastor@graceofva.org